TAPAS &
MINI BITES

✐ LAKELAND

Lakeland and ACP Magazines Ltd hereby exclude all liability to the extent permitted by law for any errors or omission in this book and for any loss, damage or expense (whether direct or indirect) suffered by a third party relying on any information contained in this book.

This book was created in 2013 for Lakeland by AWW Books, an imprint of Octopus Publishing Group Ltd, based on materials licensed to it by ACP Magazines Ltd, a division of Nine Entertainment Co.

54 Park St, Sydney
GPO Box 4088, Sydney, NSW 2001.
phone (02) 9282 8618; fax (02) 9126 3702
acpbooks@acpmagazines.com.au;
www.acpbooks.com.au

OCTOPUS PUBLISHING GROUP
Design – Chris Bell
Food Director – Pamela Clark

Published for Lakeland in the United Kingdom by Octopus Publishing Group Limited

Endeavour House
189 Shaftesbury Avenue
London WC2H 8JY
United Kingdom
phone + 44 (0) 207 632 5400;
fax + 44 (0) 207 632 5405
aww@octopusbooks.co.uk;
www.octopusbooks.co.uk
www.australian-womens-weekly.com

Printed and bound in China

A catalogue record for this book is available from the British Library.

ISBN 978-1-907428-87-6

The Department of Health advises that eggs should not be consumed raw. This book contains some dishes made with raw or lightly cooked eggs. It is prudent for vulnerable people such as pregnant and nursing mothers, invalids, the elderly, babies and young children to avoid uncooked or lightly cooked dishes made with eggs. Once prepared, these dishes should be kept refrigerated and used promptly.

This book also includes dishes made with nuts and nut derivatives. It is advisable for those with known allergic reactions to nuts and nut derivatives and those who may be potentially vulnerable to these allergies, such as pregnant and nursing mothers, invalids, the elderly, babies and children to avoid dishes made with nuts and nut oils. It is also prudent to check the labels of pre-prepared ingredients for the possible inclusion of nut derivatives.

Some of the recipes in this book have appeared in other publications.

TAPAS &
MINI BITES

Entertain in style with this collection of over 50 mouth-watering recipes for tapas, nibbles and party snacks, both savoury and sweet. From Wasabi Salmon and Leek & Brie Tartlets to Dolmades and Mini Toffee Apples, there are tempting bite-sized morsels for every occasion from casual get-togethers with friends to special family celebrations.

One of an exciting new series of cookbooks from Lakeland, *Tapas & Mini Bites* is packed with delicious colour photos plus expert hints, tips and techniques for beginners and experienced cooks alike.

With every recipe triple-tested® for perfect results, these excellent cookbooks are sure to become some of the best-loved on your kitchen bookshelf. To discover the rest of the range, together with our unrivalled selection of creative kitchenware, visit one of our friendly Lakeland stores or shop online at www.lakeland.co.uk.

CONTENTS

PARTY PLANNING

Serving tapas and finger food is a great way to entertain – informal, convivial and offering a wide range of delicious choices. With a little planning and preparation, you can relax and enjoy the festivities.

TERRIFIC TAPAS

Traditionally served in Spanish bars, tapas are small dishes of food that can you can mix and match to enjoy either as an accompaniment to pre-dinner drinks or as an entire meal. For a delicious feast, serve a selection of tapas with plenty of fresh, crusty bread, olives and a jug of sangria.

CHOICE OF FOOD

It's a good idea to serve a mix of hot and cold dishes, but it is better to have fewer dishes that go well together than to be over-ambitious and have too many.

When choosing what to serve, things to consider are the time of year – you may want light dishes in summer and more robust options in winter – how many people will be there, the occasion, and how much time and help you have at your disposal.

If you are planning a buffet or cocktail party, aim for a range of complementary colours, textures, flavours and ingredients. You could also consider having a theme – Italian or Middle Eastern,

for example. If the mini bites and tapas are a prelude to a meal, opt for a few tasty items that are not too filling.

HOW MUCH FOOD?

You don't want to overdo it but you do want all your guests to have plenty of food to enjoy. Here are some guidelines:

For pre-dinner nibbles: allow 4–5 mini bites per person.

For a cocktail party: allow 4–5 mini bites for per person for the first hour and around 4 per person for every hour after that.

For a full afternoon or evening: allow 12–14 mini bites per person.

For tapas: aim to create around 5–6 dishes, perhaps 3 hot and 3 cold, based on a variety of ingredients. To accompany pre-dinner drinks, calculate 3–4 helpings per person, for a cocktail party 6–8 helpings and, if the tapas are making up a complete meal, calculate on 12–15 helpings per person.

For sweet mini bites: base your catering numbers on guests having 2–3 of these mini desserts.

MAKING IT ALL STRESS-FREE

Whatever the occasion, try to do as much ahead as possible. If you can, make some of the dishes long in advance and freeze them and, if you are really pressed for time, here a few shortcuts:

• Head for the deli counter at the supermarket and stock up on cheese and antipasti which can be attractively arranged on a platter in minutes.

• Present shop-bought dips in pretty serving bowls accompanied with a selection of crunchy vegetables, crackers and crisps for dipping.

• Cold meats and seafood are also easily arranged on large platters and look impressive with almost no effort.

• Use bottled ingredients, like pesto or tapenade, rather than making your own.

PARTY CHECKLIST

Here's a list of some of the items you may need to remember for your party:

• Cutlery
• Plates (paper or china)
• Glasses or plastic cups
• Serving trays and platters
• Serving bowls
• Serving spoons
• Napkins
• Bin bags
• Extra fridge and freezer space
• Oven trays
• Airtight storage containers
• Ice

DRINKS

When buying alcohol, plan for about 4 drinks per person. Don't forget to include some beer and soft drinks for those who are not too keen on wine or spirits. If this sounds a little daunting or expensive, remember you can always delegate each guest or group to bring a bottle of alcohol or a mixer. Remember who is bringing what, otherwise you may end up with 6 bottles of one thing and none of another.

TAPAS

COD & OLIVE FRITTERS

650g salt cod fillet, skin on
3 medium potatoes (600g),
    halved
1 tablespoon olive oil
1 medium brown onion (150g),
    chopped finely
2 cloves garlic, crushed
3 tablespoons finely chopped
    fresh flat-leaf parsley
60g pitted green olives,
    chopped finely
1 egg
vegetable oil, for deep-frying

1 Rinse fish under cold water to remove excess salt. Place fish in large bowl, cover with cold water; refrigerate, covered, overnight, changing the water three or four times. Drain fish; discard water.
2 Place fish in large saucepan, cover with cold water; bring to the boil uncovered. Reduce heat, simmer, covered, 5 minutes. Drain fish, discard water; remove skin and bones then flake fish.
3 Boil, steam or microwave potato until tender; drain. Roughly mash potato in large bowl.
4 Meanwhile, heat olive oil in large frying pan; cook onion and garlic, stirring, until onion softens.
5 Combine fish, onion mixture, parsley, olives and egg with potato; mix well.
6 Roll level tablespoons of fish mixture into balls, place on baking-parchment-lined tray; refrigerate 30 minutes.
7 Heat vegetable oil in deep medium saucepan; deep-fry fritters, in batches, until browned lightly and heated through. Drain on absorbent paper.

prep + cook time 1 hour
30 minutes + refrigeration time
makes 40
nutritional count per fritter
2.6g fat; 196kJ (47 cal)
tip Salt cod, also known as baccalà, bacalhau, bacalao and morue, is available from Italian, Spanish, Portuguese and Jamaican delicatessans and online. It needs to be de-salted and rehydrated before use.

DEEP-FRIED WHITEBAIT

150g plain flour
3 tablespoons coarsely chopped
 fresh coriander
500g whitebait
vegetable oil, for deep-frying

cucumber garlic dip
20g ghee
½ teaspoon ground coriander
½ teaspoon ground cumin
210g natural yogurt
½ cucumber (130g), deseeded,
 chopped finely
1 clove garlic, crushed
1 tablespoon lemon juice

1 Make cucumber garlic dip.
2 Combine flour and coriander
in large bowl; add whitebait, in
batches, toss until coated.
3 Heat oil in medium saucepan;
deep-fry whitebait, in batches,
until browned and cooked
through. Drain on absorbent
paper. Serve with cucumber garlic
dip.

cucumber garlic dip Heat ghee
in small saucepan; cook ground
spices, stirring, until fragrant, cool.
Combine yogurt, cucumber, garlic
and juice in small bowl for dip; stir
in spice mixture.

prep + cook time 45 minutes
serves 4
nutritional count per serving
35.4g fat; 2337kJ (559 cal)

POTATO, DILL & PRAWN TORTILLA

30g butter
2 teaspoons olive oil
2 medium potatoes (400g),
   chopped finely
1 medium brown onion (150g),
   chopped finely
12 uncooked medium king
   prawns (540g)
6 eggs
2 tablespoons soured cream
2 tablespoons finely chopped
   fresh dill

1 Preheat oven to 200°C/180°C fan-assisted.
2 Heat butter and oil in medium frying pan; cook potato, stirring occasionally, 5 minutes. Add onion; cook, stirring occasionally, until potato is browned and tender.
3 Meanwhile, shell and devein prawns; add to pan with potato. Cook until prawns change colour.
4 Whisk eggs with soured cream in medium bowl until smooth; stir in dill. Pour mixture into pan; stir gently. Cook tortilla over low heat, about 10 minutes or until bottom sets. Wrap pan handle in foil; place pan in oven. Cook tortilla, uncovered, about 15 minutes or until tortilla is set and browned.
5 Stand tortilla 10 minutes before cutting into bite size pieces; serve warm.

prep + cook time 45 minutes
serves 10
nutritional count per serving 8.3g fat; 589kJ (141 cal)

SHERRY-GLAZED CHICKEN LIVERS

1 tablespoon olive oil
500g chicken livers, trimmed,
   sliced thinly
20g butter
2 shallots (50g), chopped finely
80ml dry sherry
125ml chicken stock
2 small long crusty bread rolls,
   each cut into 6 slices
30g watercress
1 teaspoon sherry vinegar

1 Heat oil in large frying pan; add liver, stir over high heat about 1 minute or until liver is barely cooked. Remove from pan; cover to keep warm.
2 Add butter and shallot to same pan; cook, stirring, until shallot softens.
3 Add sherry to pan; simmer until liquid is reduced by half. Add stock; simmer until liquid is slightly thickened. Return liver to pan; stir until heated.
4 Toast bread rolls lightly both sides.
5 Spoon liver mixture over toast; sprinkle watercress with vinegar. Top toasts with watercress mixture.

prep + cook time 30 minutes
makes 12
nutritional count per piece
4.9g fat; 464kJ (111 cal)

VEAL MEATBALLS WITH GAZPACHO SALSA

1 tablespoon olive oil
1 large brown onion (200g),
  chopped finely
2 cloves garlic, crushed
500g minced veal
2 tablespoons finely chopped
  fresh oregano
120g manchego cheese,
  grated finely
70g stale breadcrumbs
1 egg
vegetable oil, for shallow-frying

gazpacho salsa
½ cucumber (130g), deseeded,
  chopped finely
1 medium green pepper (200g),
  chopped finely
½ small red onion (50g), chopped
  finely
1 small tomato (30g), deseeded,
  chopped finely
2 tablespoons olive oil
1 tablespoon sherry vinegar

1 Make gazpacho salsa.
2 Heat olive oil in medium frying
pan; cook onion and garlic,
stirring, until onion softens. Cool
5 minutes.
3 Combine onion mixture, veal,
oregano, cheese, breadcrumbs
and egg in large bowl. Roll
rounded tablespoons of the veal
mixture into balls.
4 Heat vegetable oil in large
frying pan; shallow-fry meatballs,
in batches, until cooked through.
Drain on absorbent paper. Serve
hot with gazpacho salsa.

gazpacho salsa Combine
ingredients in small bowl.

prep + cook time 50 minutes
makes 40
nutritional count per meatball
4.1g fat; 247kJ (59 cal)
tip You can use parmesan cheese
instead, if manchego is not
available.

FENNEL & GARLIC ROASTED PORK RIBS

1 tablespoon fennel seeds
90g tomato paste
1 tablespoon brown sugar
60ml sherry vinegar
4 cloves garlic, crushed
2 teaspoons smoked paprika
60ml olive oil
2 x 500g racks pork spare ribs

1 Combine seeds, tomato paste, sugar, vinegar, garlic, paprika and oil in medium jug. Reserve 60ml of the marinade. Place pork in shallow dish, pour over marinade; turn pork to coat in marinade. Cover; refrigerate 1 hour.
2 Preheat oven to 200°C/180°C fan-assisted.
3 Place pork on oiled wire rack over large baking dish; roast, uncovered, 30 minutes.
4 Increase oven temperature to 220°C/200°C fan-assisted. Brush pork with reserved marinade; roast about 20 minutes or until cooked through.
5 Slice ribs between the bones; serve with lemon wedges, if you like.

prep + cook time 1 hour + refrigeration time
serves 6
nutritional count per serving 15.2g fat; 915kJ (219 cal)

LEMON, CHORIZO & CHICKEN SKEWERS

400g chicken breast fillets, cut
  into 2cm pieces
340g chorizo sausage, cut into
  2cm pieces
1 medium yellow pepper (200g),
  cut into 2cm pieces
12 bay leaves
1 tablespoon finely grated
  lemon rind
1 tablespoon lemon juice
60ml olive oil
2 cloves garlic, crushed
1 teaspoon dried chilli flakes
3 tablespoons finely chopped
  fresh flat-leaf parsley

1 Combine ingredients in large
bowl; cover and refrigerate for
30 minutes.
2 Thread chicken, chorizo, pepper
and bay leaves, alternately, onto
skewers.
3 Cook skewers on heated oiled
griddle pan until chicken is cooked
through and chorizo is browned
lightly.

prep + cook time 30 minutes
+ refrigeration time
makes 12
nutritional count per skewer
15.3g fat; 832kJ (199 cal)
tip Soak 12 bamboo skewers in
water for at least an hour before
using to prevent them from
scorching during cooking.

BROAD BEANS & THYME

600g frozen broad beans, thawed
10g butter
2 shallots (50g), chopped finely
150g speck, chopped finely
1 tablespoon fresh thyme leaves
1 tablespoon lemon juice

1 Drop beans into medium saucepan of boiling water, return to the boil; drain. When beans are cool enough to handle, peel away grey-coloured outer shells.
2 Heat butter in large frying pan; cook shallot and speck, stirring, until speck is browned lightly. Add beans and thyme; cook, stirring, until beans are heated through. Stir in juice.

prep + cook time 40 minutes
serves 4
nutritional count per serving 7.7g fat; 589kJ (141 cal)
tip Speck is an uncooked, dry-cured and aged ham traditionally from the Tyrol. If you can't find it, use prosciutto or smoked bacon instead.

ANCHOVY & GOAT'S CHEESE
BAKED MUSHROOMS

20 large button mushrooms
  (400g)
120g stale breadcrumbs
120g soft goat's cheese
60ml olive oil
4 drained anchovy fillets,
  chopped finely
4 tablespoons finely chopped
  fresh chives
250ml chicken stock

1 Preheat oven to 200°C/180°C fan-assisted.
2 Remove and discard stems from mushrooms; place mushroom caps, in single layer, in medium baking dish.
3 Combine breadcrumbs, cheese, oil, anchovy and chives in medium bowl. Stuff mushrooms with mixture.
4 Add stock to baking dish; bake, uncovered, about 15 minutes or until mushrooms are browned lightly.

prep + cook time 40 minutes
makes 20
nutritional count per mushroom
4.1g fat; 276kJ (66 cal)

ROSEMARY POTATOES WITH LEEK & CHORIZO

500g baby new potatoes, sliced
   thickly
340g chorizo sausage, cut into
   1cm thick slices
1 large leek (500g), trimmed,
   chopped coarsely
6 cloves garlic
1 tablespoon finely chopped
   fresh rosemary
2 teaspoons sweet paprika
5 bay leaves
60ml olive oil

1 Preheat oven to 220°C/200°C fan-assisted.
2 Combine ingredients in large baking dish. Roast, uncovered, about 30 minutes or until potatoes are browned lightly.

prep + cook time 45 minutes
serves 8
nutritional count per serving
19.8g fat; 1120kJ (268 cal)

AUBERGINE FRITTERS

2 large aubergines (1kg)
100g mozzarella cheese, grated
  coarsely
6 tablespoons coarsely chopped
  fresh flat-leaf parsley
2 cloves garlic, crushed
50g packaged breadcrumbs
35g plain flour
2 eggs
vegetable oil, for shallow-frying

1 Preheat oven to 220°C/200°C fan-assisted.
2 Remove and discard stem ends from aubergines; prick aubergines all over with fork. Place on oiled oven tray; roast, uncovered, about 30 minutes or until soft. Cool. Peel aubergines; chop flesh finely.
3 Combine aubergine, cheese, parsley, garlic, breadcrumbs, flour and eggs in large bowl. Using wetted hands, shape level tablespoons of mixture into oval patties.
4 Heat oil in large frying pan; cook fritters, in batches, until browned both sides. Drain on absorbent paper. Serve with lemon wedges, if you like.

prep + cook time 1 hour
makes 36
nutritional count per fritter
5.3g fat; 272kJ (65 cal)
tip Fritters can be served warm or cold.

TO SHARE

SMOKED TROUT DIP

1 medium potato (200g),
  chopped coarsely
60ml warm milk
150g piece smoked trout, flaked
1 clove garlic, crushed
2 tablespoons olive oil
2 spring onions, chopped finely

1 Boil, steam or microwave potato until tender; drain. Push potato through fine sieve into small bowl; stir in milk.
2 Combine trout, garlic, oil and onion in medium bowl; fold in potato mixture.
3 Serve dip with crackers or crusty bread.

prep + cook time 30 minutes
makes 375ml
nutritional count per teaspoon 0.7g fat; 46kJ (11 cal)

FETA & OLIVE DIP WITH GARLIC TOAST

40g pitted whole green olives
200g feta cheese
1 clove garlic, quartered
200g natural yogurt
2 tablespoons finely chopped
    green olives
1 loaf ciabatta bread
2 tablespoons olive oil
2 cloves garlic, crushed

1 Blend or process whole olives, cheese, quartered garlic and yogurt until smooth. Transfer to small serving bowl; stir in chopped olives.

2 Cut bread into 18 slices. Brush bread with combined oil and crushed garlic; grill bread slices until browned both sides. Halve toasts diagonally; serve with dip.

prep + cook time 25 minutes
serves 6
nutritional count per serving
17.9g fat; 1668kJ (399 cal)
tip Dip can be kept, covered, in the refrigerator for up to 1 week.

WHITE BEAN DIP

1 tablespoon olive oil

1 medium leek (350g), sliced thinly

400g can white beans, rinsed, drained

300ml double cream

1 teaspoon finely grated lemon rind

1 tablespoon lemon juice

2 tablespoons finely chopped fresh flat-leaf parsley

1 Heat oil in small frying pan; cook leek, stirring, about 10 minutes or until leek softens. Allow to cool.

2 Blend or process leek, beans, cream, rind and juice until smooth. Stir in parsley.

3 Serve dip with crackers or crusty bread.

prep + cook time 25 minutes
makes 625ml
nutritional count per teaspoon 1.2g fat; 59kJ (14 cal)
tip We used cannellini beans in this recipe but you can use any white bean you like.

THREE DELICIOUS DIPS

BASIL DIP

100g fresh basil leaves
160ml olive oil
1 clove garlic, quartered
2 teaspoons finely grated lemon
   rind
2 tablespoons finely grated
   parmesan cheese

1 Blend or process ingredients
until smooth.

prep time 5 minutes
makes 250ml
nutritional count per teaspoon
3.1g fat; 121kJ (29 cal)

OLIVE DIP

300g large black olives, pitted
2 tablespoons rinsed, drained
   capers
1 clove garlic, quartered
2 tablespoons lemon juice
1 tablespoon finely chopped fresh
   flat-leaf parsley
80ml olive oil

1 Blend or process ingredients
until smooth.

prep time 10 minutes
makes 375ml
nutritional count per teaspoon
1.1g fat; 59kJ (14 cal)

ANCHOVY DIP

40 anchovy fillets, rinsed, drained
80ml olive oil
1 tablespoon lemon juice
2 cloves garlic, quartered
3 teaspoons fresh lemon thyme
   leaves
2 tablespoons boiling water

1 Blend or process anchovies,
oil, juice, garlic and thyme until
smooth.
2 Transfer to small bowl; stir in the
boiling water.

prep time 5 minutes
makes 250ml
nutritional count per teaspoon
1.8g fat; 84kJ (20 cal)

tip Serve the dips with fresh
or lightly cooked vegetables,
breadsticks or crackers.

from top to bottom: Basil dip,
Olive dip, Anchovy dip

GARLIC PIZZA WEDGES

250ml warm water
1 teaspoon caster sugar
7g sachet dried yeast
375g plain flour
1 teaspoon salt
1 tablespoon olive oil
2 cloves garlic, crushed
2 tablespoons finely grated
   parmesan cheese

1 Combine the water, sugar and yeast in small jug. Stand in warm place about 10 minutes or until frothy.
2 Sift flour and salt into large bowl. Add yeast mixture; mix to a soft dough. Knead dough on floured surface about 10 minutes or until smooth and elastic. Place dough in oiled large bowl; cover. Stand in warm place about 1 hour or until dough is doubled in size.
3 Preheat oven to 220°C/200°C fan-assisted. Grease two oven or pizza trays.
4 Divide dough in half. Roll each portion into a 30cm round; place on trays.
5 Brush pizza bases with combined oil and garlic; sprinkle with cheese.
6 Bake pizzas about 20 minutes or until browned and crisp. Cut each pizza into 16 wedges.

prep + cook time 1 hour + standing time
makes 32
nutritional count per wedge 0.9g fat; 209kJ (50 cal)
tip This recipe makes a good accompaniment for the dips in this chapter.

DUKKAH

150g sesame seeds
55g whole blanched almonds
50g pistachios
4 tablespoons ground coriander
3 tablespoons ground cumin
1 teaspoon salt
½ teaspoon freshly ground
   black pepper

1 Preheat oven to 220°C/200°C fan-assisted.
2 Roast the sesame seeds, almonds and pistachios, separately, about 10 minutes or until browned lightly. Cool.
3 Blend or process nuts until fine; transfer to medium bowl. Add seeds, coriander, cumin, salt and pepper to nut mixture; mix well. Store in an airtight container.
4 Serve the dukkah with a loaf of ciabatta or crusty bread, along with a bowl of extra virgin olive oil, for dipping bread.

prep + cook time 45 minutes
makes about 275 ml
nutritional count per tablespoon
5.8g fat; 272kJ (65 cal)
tip Dukkah originated in Egypt; it is a blend of roasted nuts and spices. It's also delicious used as a crunchy coating for chicken or fish dishes.

OLIVES FOUR WAYS

FENNEL, MINT & ORANGE OLIVES

1 Combine 120g pitted black olives, 1 trimmed, thinly sliced baby fennel bulb, 6 tablespoons fresh mint leaves, 2 tablespoons finely grated orange rind, 1 teaspoon black peppercorns and 375ml olive oil in medium bowl.
2 Cover, refrigerate overnight or up to 1 week.

prep time 15 minutes
+ refrigeration time
serves 8
nutritional count per serving
42.9g fat; 1689kJ (404 cal)

PERI-PERI OLIVES

1 Combine 150g pitted kalamata olives, 1 tablespoon finely grated lemon rind, 2 halved fresh small red chillies, 2 garlic cloves, 60ml red wine vinegar and 180ml olive oil in medium bowl.
2 Cover, refrigerate overnight or up to 1 week.

prep time 15 minutes
+ refrigeration time
serves 8
nutritional count per serving
21.6g fat; 899kJ (215 cal)

OLIVES WITH CAPERBERRIES & SHERRY VINEGAR

1 Combine 150g green queen olives, 175g rinsed drained caperberries, 5 sprigs fresh lemon thyme, 60ml sherry vinegar and 180ml olive oil in medium bowl.
2 Cover, refrigerate overnight or up to 1 week.

prep time 15 minutes
+ refrigeration time
serves 8
nutritional count per serving
21.6g fat; 932kJ (223 cal)

MARTINI OLIVES

1 Rinse and drain 370ml anchovy-stuffed green olives; combine in medium bowl with 1 tablespoon finely chopped fresh rosemary, 4 bay leaves, 1 tablespoon extra dry vermouth, 1 tablespoon gin and 125ml olive oil.
2 Cover, refrigerate overnight or up to 1 week.

prep time 15 minutes
+ refrigeration time
serves 8
nutritional count per serving
17.3g fat; 711kJ (170 cal)

clockwise from top left: Fennel, mint & orange olives, Peri-peri olives, Martini olives, Olives with caperberries & sherry vinegar

BAKED BRIE

200g whole brie
1 sprig fresh thyme
2 tablespoons dry red wine
1 teaspoon finely grated
   lemon rind
1 fresh thyme sprig, chopped
   finely

1 Preheat oven to 200°C/180°C fan-assisted.
2 Grease 250ml ovenproof dish (10cm diameter, 4cm deep). Place brie in dish. Make six small slits into cheese.
3 Cut thyme sprig fresh into six pieces; push thyme into slits. Pour wine over cheese; cover dish, place on oven tray.
4 Bake about 20 minutes. Stand, covered, 5 minutes.
5 Sprinkle with rind and chopped thyme and serve with chunks of crusty bread or breadsticks.

prep + cook time 40 minutes
serves 8
nutritional count per serving
7.3g fat; 368kJ (88 cal)

HOT MINI BITES

PEPPER & TOMATO SOUP WITH BASIL PESTO

2 medium red peppers (400g)
4 medium tomatoes (600g),
    halved
1 fresh long red chilli, halved
    lengthways
5 unpeeled cloves garlic
500ml chicken stock

basil pesto
1 large handful fresh basil leaves
1½ tablespoons finely grated
    parmesan cheese
1 tablespoon lemon juice
1 tablespoon roasted pine nuts
2 tablespoons olive oil

1 Preheat oven to 240°C/220°C fan-assisted.
2 Quarter peppers; discard seeds and membranes. Place quarters, skin-side up, on oiled oven tray with tomatoes, cut-side up, and chilli and garlic. Roast, uncovered, about 20 minutes or until pepper skin blisters and blackens and vegetables are soft.
3 Cover vegetables with foil, stand 10 minutes; peel away skin.
4 Reserve one garlic clove for pesto. Blend vegetables and stock until smooth; strain.
5 Meanwhile, make basil pesto.
6 Reheat soup in medium saucepan. Divide soup into shot glasses; top each with tiny amount of pesto. Garnish with chilli curls.

basil pesto Blend reserved garlic, basil, cheese, juice and nuts until chopped. With motor operating, gradually add oil in a thin stream until smooth.

prep + cook time 55 minutes
+ standing time
serves 30
nutritional count per serving
1.8g fat; 102kJ (24cal)
tips Make chilli curls by slicing a long red chilli thinly lengthways. Place strips in iced water for about 10 minutes. Soup and pesto can be made up to 1 month ahead and frozen separately. Thaw soup and pesto in refrigerator overnight. Reheat soup; pesto might need a little oil stirred through for a good consistency.

GREEK MEATBALLS

1 tablespoon olive oil

1 medium brown onion (150g), chopped finely

2 cloves garlic, crushed

1kg lean minced lamb

1 egg

100g stale breadcrumbs

2 tablespoons lemon juice

3 tablespoons finely chopped fresh flat-leaf parsley

3 tablespoons finely chopped fresh mint

50g plain flour

olive oil, extra, for shallow-frying

1 Heat oil in medium frying pan, add onion and garlic; cook, stirring, until onion is softened. Cool.

2 Combine onion mixture with mince, egg, breadcrumbs, juice, parsley and mint in large bowl. Cover, refrigerate 1 hour.

3 Roll level tablespoons of mixture into balls; toss balls in flour, shake away excess. Heat extra oil in same cleaned pan; shallow-fry meatballs, in batches, until cooked through. Drain on absorbent paper.

4 Serve meatballs with natural yogurt, if you like.

prep + cook time 1 hour + refrigeration time
makes 50
nutritional count per meatball 4.7g fat; 297kJ (71 cal)
tips The oil should be very hot before cooking the meatballs. Minced beef or veal can also be used in this recipe.

BEEF & STILTON PIES

2 tablespoons vegetable oil
500g stewing beef, cut into 1cm
    cubes
1 medium brown onion (150g),
    chopped finely
1 clove garlic, crushed
2 tablespoons tomato paste
1 tablespoon plain flour
60ml dry red wine
500ml beef stock
5 sheets ready-rolled shortcrust
    pastry
100g stilton cheese, crumbled
1 egg
1 tablespoon milk

1 Heat half the oil in medium saucepan; cook beef in batches until browned. Heat remaining oil in same pan; cook onion and garlic until soft.

2 Return beef to pan with tomato paste, stir over heat until combined. Add flour; cook, stirring until mixture bubbles. Stir in wine, then gradually add stock; continue stirring until mixture boils and thickens. Reduce heat; simmer, covered, about 45 minutes or until beef is tender. Cool.

3 Meanwhile, cut 48 x 6.5cm rounds as close together as possible from all the pastry sheets; line two 24-hole mini muffin pans. Prick the base of each pastry case with a fork.

4 Preheat oven to 220°C/200°C fan-assisted.

5 Fill each case with rounded teaspoons of beef mixture; top with a small piece of cheese.

6 Cut out 48 x 4.5cm rounds from remaining pastry scraps. Combine egg and milk in a small bowl; brush around inside top edge of each pastry case with egg mixture, cover with pastry rounds, press

edges together. Brush pies with more egg mixture; cut a hole in each pie to allow steam to escape.

7 Bake pies about 20 minutes or until golden. Stand pies in pan 5 minutes before serving.

prep + cook time 1 hour 45 minutes
makes 48
nutritional count per pie 6.9g fat; 472kJ (113 cal)
tips Pies can be made up to 1 month ahead and frozen. Thaw in refrigerator overnight. Reheat pies in a single layer on oven trays, covered loosely with foil, in oven at 180°C/160°C fan-assisted about 10 minutes.

WASABI SALMON

650g piece salmon fillet
2 teaspoons wasabi paste
60ml japanese soy sauce
½ teaspoon sesame oil

dipping sauce
80ml rice wine vinegar
1 tablespoon white sugar
¼ cucumber (65g), deseeded,
   chopped finely

1 Using tweezers, remove fine
bones from salmon. Remove skin;
cut salmon into 2cm cubes.
2 Combine paste, sauce and oil in
medium bowl, add salmon; turn to
coat, stand 15 minutes.
3 Meanwhile, make dipping
sauce.
4 Drain salmon; discard marinade.
Heat large oiled frying pan; cook
salmon, in batches, over high heat
about 20 seconds each side. Serve
warm salmon with dipping sauce.

dipping sauce Stir ingredients in
small bowl until sugar dissolves.

prep + cook time 35 minutes
+ standing time
makes 48
nutritional count per serving
1.8g fat; 141kJ (34 cal)
tips A non-stick pan is best to
use for cooking the salmon.
Don't overcook the salmon, it
should be rare.

CHICKEN & MUSHROOM PARTY PIES

1 tablespoon olive oil

1 small brown onion (80g) chopped finely

1 clove garlic, crushed

400g minced chicken

100g mushrooms, chopped finely

2 teaspoons plain flour

180ml single cream

2 tablespoons finely chopped fresh chives

3 sheets ready-rolled shortcrust pastry

1 egg, beaten lightly

2 sheets ready-rolled puff pastry

2 teaspoons sesame seeds

1 Heat oil in medium frying pan; cook onion and garlic, stirring, until onion softens. Add chicken and mushrooms; cook, stirring, until chicken changes colour. Add flour; cook, stirring, 1 minute. Gradually stir in cream; cook, stirring, until mixture boils and thickens. Stir in chives; cool.

2 Preheat oven to 200°C/180°C fan-assisted. Grease two 12-hole (40ml) muffin pans.

3 Cut 24 x 7cm rounds from shortcrust pastry; press into pan holes. Brush edges with a little of the egg. Spoon chicken mixture into pastry cases.

4 Cut 24 x 6cm rounds from puff pastry; top pies with puff pastry lids. Press edges firmly to seal; brush lids with remaining egg, sprinkle with sesame seeds. Cut a small slit in top of each pie.

5 Bake about 20 minutes or until browned lightly. Stand pies in pan 5 minutes before serving.

prep + cook time 55 minutes
makes 24
nutritional count per pie
14.5g fat; 895kJ (214 cal)

CHICKEN TANDOORI WITH NAAN BREAD

280g natural yogurt
4 tablespoons finely chopped
  fresh coriander leaves
400g chicken breast fillets, cut
  into 1cm cubes
2 tablespoons tandoori paste
110g mango chutney

naan bread
300g plain flour
¼ teaspoon baking powder
¼ teaspoon salt
1 teaspoon dried yeast
1 teaspoon black onion seeds
95g natural yogurt
1 tablespoon vegetable oil
1 egg
80ml warm milk, approximately

1 Combine yogurt and coriander in large bowl; reserve and refrigerate 60ml for serving. Stir chicken and paste into remaining coriander yogurt; refrigerate.
2 Meanwhile, make naan bread.
3 Stir chicken mixture in heated oiled frying pan until cooked.
4 Top each naan with ¼ teaspoon mango chutney, a piece of the tandoori chicken and a dollop of reserved coriander yogurt.

naan bread Sift flour, baking powder and salt into large bowl; stir in yeast and seeds. Make a well in centre; add yogurt, oil, egg and enough milk to mix to a soft dough. Turn onto floured surface, knead 5 minutes or until smooth and elastic. Place in large oiled bowl; cover, stand in warm place 2 hours or until doubled in size. Preheat grill to highest setting. Heat a heavy-duty oven tray under grill. Cut dough in half and working with one half at a time, divide into 2cm balls. Roll balls out to 3mm thick, stretch ends of each piece of dough. Grill naan, in batches, on hot tray, 45 seconds each side or until browned.

prep + cook time 1 hour
+ standing time
makes 80
nutritional count per serving
0.8g fat; 133kJ (32 cal)
tips Naan breads can be made up to 1 week ahead and frozen. Thaw naan breads at room temperature for 4 hours. Reheat naan breads on oven trays, covered loosely with foil, in oven at 220°C/200°C fan-assisted. Assemble naan breads just before serving.

CHEESE FILO TRIANGLES

150g feta cheese, crumbled
125g ricotta cheese
1 egg, beaten lightly
¼ teaspoon ground nutmeg
½ teaspoon freshly ground
   black pepper
12 sheets filo pastry
100g butter, melted

1 Preheat oven to 180°C/160°C fan-assisted.
2 Combine feta, ricotta, egg, nutmeg and pepper in small bowl; mix well.
3 To prevent pastry from drying out, cover with cling film, then a damp tea towel while making triangles.
4 Layer two sheets of pastry, brushing both sheets with a little butter. Cut layered sheets into four strips lengthways. Place two teaspoons of cheese mixture at one end of each pastry strip. Fold one corner end of pastry diagonally across filling to other edge to form a triangle. Continue folding to end of strip, retaining triangle shape.
5 Brush triangles with a little butter. Repeat with remaining pastry, filling and butter.
6 Place triangles on greased oven trays; bake about 15 minutes or until browned.

prep + cook time 40 minutes
makes 24
nutritional count per triangle
5.8g fat; 328kJ (78 cal)
tip The uncooked triangles can be made up to 1 month ahead and frozen. There's no need to defrost them before cooking.

POTATO SKINS

5 medium potatoes (1kg),
  unpeeled
2 tablespoons olive oil
120g soured cream

1 Preheat oven to 200°C/180°C fan-assisted.
2 Scrub potatoes well; brush with half of the oil. Place potatoes on oven tray; bake, uncovered, in hot oven about 50 minutes or until tender. Cool.
3 Cut each potato into six wedges; carefully remove flesh, leaving skins intact. Place potato skins, skin-side down, on wire rack over oven tray; brush with remaining oil. Roast, uncovered, about 20 minutes or until crisp.
4 Serve potato skins with soured cream.

prep + cook time 1 hour 20 minutes + cooling time
makes 30
nutritional count per potato skin 1.2g fat; 99kJ (24 cal)
nutritional count per tablespoon soured cream 7.9g fat; 312kJ (75 cal)

tip The potatoes can be prepared several hours ahead; cook skins just before serving.

ARANCINI BALLS

625ml chicken stock
1 tablespoon olive oil
1 small brown onion (80g),
   chopped finely
1 clove garlic, crushed
200g arborio rice
125ml dry white wine
60g frozen peas
40g ham, chopped finely
40g finely grated parmesan
   cheese
60g mozzarella cheese
1 egg, beaten lightly
plain flour, for coating
1 egg, beaten lightly, extra
1 tablespoon milk
100g packaged dry breadcrumbs
vegetable oil, for deep-frying

1 Bring stock to a boil in medium saucepan. Reduce heat to low and keep hot.
2 Heat olive oil in medium saucepan, add onion and garlic; cook, stirring, until onion is soft but not coloured. Add rice; cook, stirring, 2 minutes. Add white wine; cook, stirring, until liquid has evaporated.
3 Add about 80ml of the hot stock; cook, stirring, over low heat until the liquid is absorbed. Repeat until all the stock has been used. Total cooking time will be about 25 minutes.
4 Stir in peas and ham; remove from heat, stir in parmesan. Transfer risotto to medium heatproof bowl; cool.
4 Chop mozzarella into 16 pieces. Stir egg into risotto. Roll 2-level-tablespoon portions of risotto mixture into balls; press a piece of mozzarella into centre of each ball, roll to enclose. Toss balls in flour, shake away excess flour. Dip into combined extra egg and milk, then coat in breadcrumbs.

5 Heat vegetable oil in deep saucepan; deep-fry arancini, in batches, until browned and heated through. Drain on absorbent paper.

prep + cook time 1 hour 20 minutes + cooling time
makes 16
nutritional count per arancini
8.7g fat; 664kJ (158 cal)
tip The risotto mixture can be made a day ahead.

CARAMELISED LEEK & BRIE TARTLETS

1 tablespoon olive oil
25g butter
2 medium leeks (700g), sliced
　finely
1 clove garlic, crushed
1 tablespoon brown sugar
1 tablespoon white wine vinegar
3 sheets ready-rolled puff pastry
200g brie cheese
24 sprigs lemon thyme

1 Preheat oven to 200°C/180°C fan-assisted. Grease two 12-hole (40ml) muffin pans.
2 Heat oil and butter in large frying pan; cook leek over medium heat, stirring, about 5 minutes or until leek softens. Add garlic, sugar and vinegar; cook, stirring, about 8 minutes or until leek caramelises.
3 Cut 8 squares from each pastry sheet; press one pastry square into each pan hole. Divide leek mixture among pastry cases.
4 Cut cheese into 24 slices. Place a slice of cheese and thyme sprig on top of each tartlet. Bake about 20 minutes.

prep + cook time 40 minutes
makes 24
nutritional count per tartlet
8.8g fat; 535kJ (128 cal)

SWEETCORN FRITTERS WITH ROCKET PURÉE

½ small red pepper (75g)
1 egg
125ml milk
½ small red onion (50g), chopped
  finely
160g corn kernels
1 tablespoon finely chopped
  fresh basil
75g self-raising flour
pinch bicarbonate of soda
120g soured cream

rocket purée
125g rocket
2 teaspoons olive oil

1 Make rocket purée.
2 Roast the pepper under the grill, or cook in the oven until the skin blisters and blackens, cover, cool, then remove skin. Chop the flesh finely.
3 Whisk egg and milk in large bowl, stir in vegetables and basil. Sift flour and bicarbonate of soda over vegetable mixture, stir until combined.
4 Cook rounded teaspoonfuls vegetable mixture in large oiled frying pan, over medium heat, about 2 minutes each side or until fritters are browned.
5 Top each fritter with about ½ teaspoon each of soured cream and rocket purée. Serve fritters immediately.

rocket purée Bring a small saucepan of water to the boil. Add rocket, return to the boil; drain immediately. Rinse rocket under cold water; drain. Blend rocket with oil until smooth.

prep + cook time 35 minutes
makes 48
nutritional count per fritter 1.4g fat; 101kJ (24 cal)
tips You can use fresh, frozen (then thawed) or well-drained canned kernels for this recipe. Fritters can be made up to 1 week ahead and frozen. Reheat frozen fritters in a single layer on oven trays, cover loosely with foil, in an oven preheated to 180°C/160°C fan-assisted, for about 10 minutes. Make rocket purée close to serving, it will discolour on standing; cover surface of purée with cling film.

CRISP POTATO & PEANUT CAKES

250g tapioca
1 tablespoon sunflower oil
1 teaspoon cumin seeds
¼ teaspoon ground turmeric
3 medium potatoes (600g),
    peeled, chopped coarsely
2 tablespoons finely chopped
    roasted unsalted peanuts
6 tablespoons finely chopped
    fresh coriander
2 long green chillies, chopped
    finely
4cm piece fresh ginger (20g),
    grated
sunflower oil, for shallow-frying,
    extra

tomato onion raita
1 teaspoon black mustard seeds
500g natural yogurt
2 medium tomatoes (300g),
    deseeded, chopped finely
2 spring onions, chopped finely
6 tablespoons finely chopped
    fresh coriander

1 Make tomato onion raita.
2 Place tapioca in large heatproof bowl; cover with boiling water. Stand 10 minutes; drain.
3 Meanwhile, heat oil in small frying pan; cook cumin and turmeric, stirring, until fragrant.
4 Boil, steam or microwave potato until tender; drain. Mash potato in large bowl then stir in tapioca, cumin, turmeric, nuts, coriander, chilli and ginger. Shape heaped tablespoons of potato mixture into small patties. Heat extra oil in large frying pan; shallow-fry potato cakes, in batches, until browned. Drain on absorbent paper; serve with raita.

tomato onion raita Cook mustard seeds in heated small frying pan until seeds begin to pop. Combine seeds in medium bowl with the remaining ingredients.

prep + cook time 1 hour 10 minutes
makes 36
nutritional count per cake 2g fat; 53 cal (221kJ)
nutritional count per tablespoon raita 0.4g fat; 10 cal (42kJ)

FRIED CAULIFLOWER

2 eggs
110g self-raising flour
125ml water
4 tablespoons finely chopped
   fresh coriander
vegetable oil, for deep-frying
1 small cauliflower (1kg), cut into
   small florets
280g greek-style natural yogurt

1 To make batter, whisk eggs, flour and the water in medium shallow bowl until smooth. Stir in half the coriander; season.

2 Heat oil in wok. Dip cauliflower in batter; drain off excess. Deep-fry cauliflower, in batches, until browned lightly and tender. Drain on absorbent paper.

3 Combine remaining coriander and yogurt in small bowl; season to taste. Serve cauliflower with coriander yogurt.

prep + cook time 15 minutes
serves 4
nutritional count per serving
9g fat; 1083kJ (259 cal)

COLD MINI BITES

SMOKED TROUT WITH PICKLED RED ONION ON RYE

1 teaspoon hot english mustard
1 teaspoon lemon juice
120g soured cream
200g hot-smoked trout
2 x 250g packets thinly sliced
   dark rye bread
bunch fresh dill

pickled red onion
½ small red onion (50g),
   quartered, sliced thinly
60ml white wine vinegar
2 teaspoons white sugar
½ teaspoon salt

1 Make pickled red onion.
2 Combine mustard, juice and cream in small bowl.
3 Discard skin and bones from trout; flake flesh into medium bowl.
4 Spread each slice of bread with mustard mixture; cut each slice into 6 squares.
5 Top each square with trout, drained pickled red onion and a sprig of dill. Serve immediately.

pickled red onion Place ingredients in screw-top jar; shake well. Refrigerate several hours or overnight.

prep time 30 minutes
+ refrigeration time
makes 96
nutritional count per piece 0.7g fat; 90kJ (21 cal)
tip Smoked salmon can be used in place of trout in this recipe.

RÖSTI WITH SMOKED SALMON

800g potatoes, peeled
15g butter, melted
1 tablespoon finely chopped
   fresh dill
125ml olive oil
200g crème fraîche
200g smoked salmon, sliced
dill for garnish, extra

1 Coarsely grate potatoes, squeeze out excess liquid. In medium bowl, combine potato, butter and dill.

2 Heat a little of the olive oil in large non-stick frying pan. Place an oiled 5cm-round metal cutter in pan and fill with 1 tablespoon of the potato mixture, pressing with back of spoon to flatten. Remove the cutter carefully (it will be hot) and repeat with remaining potato mixture and olive oil. Cook rösti until golden on each side; drain on absorbent paper, cool.

3 Place 1 teaspoon of crème fraîche on each rösti to serve; top with salmon and extra dill.

prep + cook time 45 minutes
makes 24
nutritional count per rösti 7.3g fat; 392kJ (94 cal)
tip The rösti can be made several hours ahead; assemble close to serving time.

PRAWN, AVOCADO & SWEET CHILLI TARTS

1 teaspoon olive oil
½ teaspoon sesame oil
500g uncooked large prawns, shelled, deveined, chopped finely
1 small avocado (200g), chopped finely
2 medium tomatoes (300g), deseeded, chopped finely
2 tablespoons sweet chilli sauce
2 teaspoons fish sauce
2 tablespoons finely chopped fresh coriander leaves
1 tablespoon lime juice
30 readymade filo or shortcrust mini pastry cases
30 fresh coriander leaves, extra

1 Heat oils in medium frying pan; cook prawns, stirring, over medium heat until changed in colour. Transfer prawns to heatproof bowl; cool.
2 Add avocado, tomato, sauces, chopped coriander and juice to prawns; mix gently.
3 Divide prawn mixture into pastry cases, top with extra coriander leaves.

prep + cook time 35 minutes
makes 30
nutritional count per tart 1.6g fat; 280kJ (67 cal)

OYSTERS WITH LIME & CORIANDER

24 oysters, on the half shell
60ml lime juice
1 teaspoon Tabasco sauce
2 tablespoons finely chopped
   fresh coriander
2 spring onions, sliced thinly
1 tablespoon groundnut oil
1 clove garlic, crushed
1 teaspoon brown sugar

1 Remove oysters from shells; wash and dry shells. Return oysters to shells; place on serving platter.
2 Combine remaining ingredients in screw-top jar; shake well. Divide dressing among oysters.

prep time 10 minutes
makes 24
nutritional count per oyster
1g fat; 67kJ (16 cal)
tip Dressing can be made a day ahead; keep, covered, in the refrigerator.

RICOTTA-STUFFED PROSCIUTTO & MELON

½ medium cantaloupe melon
   (850g)
5 slices prosciutto (75g)
150g ricotta cheese
1 tablespoon finely chopped
   fresh chives
2 tablespoons finely chopped
   roasted walnuts

1 Peel melon; cut lengthways into 10 slices. Cut each slice in half crossways.
2 Cut each slice prosciutto in half lengthways; cut each slice in half crossways.
3 Combine remaining ingredients in small bowl.
4 Spread cheese mixture over one side of each prosciutto; wrap prosciutto firmly around melon.

prep time 20 minutes
makes 20
nutritional count per piece
1.8g fat; 121kJ (29 cal)
tip You could use halved fresh figs instead of the cantaloupe melon, if you like.

SMOKED CHICKEN SALAD ON BLINI

50g buckwheat flour
2 tablespoons plain flour
½ teaspoon baking powder
1 egg
125ml buttermilk
20g butter, melted
100g smoked chicken, shredded
1 small green apple (130g),
    chopped finely
2 spring onions, sliced thinly
75g mayonnaise
2 teaspoons wholegrain mustard
1 tablespoon coarsely chopped
    fresh chives

1 Sift flours and baking powder into small bowl, gradually whisk in combined egg and buttermilk until mixture is smooth; stir in butter.
2 Cook blini, in batches, by dropping 2 teaspoons of batter into heated large non-stick frying pan; cook blini until browned both sides. Cool on wire racks.
3 Meanwhile, reserve the chives and combine remaining ingredients in medium bowl.
4 Place blini on serving platter; divide chicken salad among blini then sprinkle with chives.

prep + cook time 30 minutes
makes 24
nutritional count per piece
2.2g fat; 171kJ (41 cal)
tip Buckwheat flour has a sweet, nutty taste and is gluten-free. It is available from some supermarkets, health food stores and online.

PARMESAN SCONES WITH GOAT'S CHEESE & TAPENADE

225g self-raising flour
30g butter
30g finely grated parmesan
  cheese
180ml buttermilk, approximately
180g goat's cheese
bunch fresh flat-leaf parsley

tapenade
200g pitted black olives
1 tablespoon rinsed drained
  capers
1 clove garlic, quartered
6 tablespoons coarsely chopped
  fresh flat-leaf parsley
5 drained anchovy fillets
1 tablespoon lemon juice
1 tablespoon olive oil

1 Preheat oven to 200°C/180°C fan-assisted. Oil oven tray.
2 Sift flour into large bowl; rub in butter, then stir in parmesan. Using a knife, mix in enough buttermilk to make a soft dough.
3 Turn dough onto floured surface, knead lightly until smooth. Press dough out to 1.5cm thickness, cut out 30 x 3cm rounds.
4 Place scones, barely touching each other, on tray. Bake about 20 minutes. Turn scones onto wire rack, cover, cool.
5 Meanwhile, make tapenade.
6 Split scones in half, top each half with tapenade and goat's cheese; top each with a parsley leaf.

tapenade Process ingredients until chopped coarsely.

prep + cook time 45 minutes
makes 60
nutritional count per scone
2.3g fat; 167kJ (40 cal)
tips Good quality tapenade is easy to buy if you don't want to make your own. Scones can be made up to 1 month ahead, wrapped in foil and frozen. Reheat frozen, foil-wrapped scones on oven tray, at 180°C/160°C fan-assisted, for about 10 minutes. Tapenade can be made up to 1 week ahead; store in the refrigerator in an airtight container, covered with a layer of olive oil.

MINI COURGETTE FRITTATAS

8 eggs
240g soured cream
3 tablespoons finely chopped
  fresh chives
2 large green courgettes (300g),
  grated coarsely
25g finely grated parmesan
  cheese
2 tablespoons coarsely chopped
  fresh chives, extra

1 Preheat oven to 180°C/160°C fan-assisted. Lightly oil four 12-hole mini muffin pans.
2 Whisk eggs with two-thirds of the soured cream in large bowl until smooth; stir in chives, courgette and cheese.
3 Divide mixture among holes of prepared pans. Bake, uncovered, 15 minutes; turn onto wire rack to cool.
4 Top frittatas with remaining soured cream and extra chives. Serve at room temperature.

prep + cook time 25 minutes
makes 48
nutritional count per frittata
3.1g fat; 142kJ (34 cal)
tips You need four 12-hole non-stick mini (30ml) muffin pans for this recipe. If you do not own that many, make the frittatas in batches, placing the cooked ones on a wire rack while you make the remainder. Frittatas can be made a day ahead and stored, covered, in the refrigerator.

OAT CAKES WITH CHEDDAR & FIG JAM

90g rolled oats
100g chilled butter, chopped coarsely
75g wholemeal plain flour
2 tablespoons plain flour
¼ teaspoon bicarbonate of soda
1½ tablespoons brown sugar
1 tablespoon milk
200g mature cheddar cheese

fig jam
3 large fresh figs (240g), chopped finely
2 tablespoons caster sugar
1 teaspoon finely grated orange rind
2 tablespoons orange juice

1 Make fig jam.
2 Preheat oven to 170°C/150°C fan-assisted. Grease oven trays.
3 Process oats until chopped finely. Add butter and sifted dry ingredients; pulse until crumbly. Add milk; process until mixture comes together. Turn dough onto floured surface, knead gently until smooth.
4 Divide dough in half; roll each half between sheets of baking parchment until 3mm thick. Cut dough into 3cm squares. Using spatula, carefully place oat cakes on trays.
5 Bake oat cakes 10 minutes or until golden brown. Cool on trays 5 minutes; transfer to wire racks to cool completely. Serve oat cakes topped with jam and a small piece of cheese.

fig jam Stir ingredients in small saucepan over low heat for about 10 minutes or until thick; cool. Transfer jam to small bowl; cover, refrigerate.

prep + cook time 45 minutes
makes 80
nutritional count per piece
1g fat; 134kJ (32 cal)
tips The jam can be made up to 1 week ahead; cover and store in the refrigerator. The oat cakes can be made 1 week in advance; store in an airtight container. If oat cakes soften, re-crisp in the oven for a few minutes, just before serving.

MINI BAKED HERB RICOTTA

250g ricotta cheese
1 egg
1 tablespoon finely chopped
  fresh flat-leaf parsley
1 teaspoon finely chopped
  fresh thyme
1 clove garlic, crushed

1 Preheat oven to 180°C/160°C fan-assisted. Oil 18 holes of two 12-hole (20ml) mini muffin pans.
2 Blend or process ingredients until smooth. Divide mixture among pan holes. Bake about 20 minutes or until browned lightly. Serve cold.

prep + cook time 30 minutes
makes 18
nutritional count per ricotta
1.9g fat; 105kJ (25 cal)
tip Baked ricotta can be made a day ahead; store, covered, in the refrigerator.

DOLMADES

2 tablespoons olive oil

2 medium brown onions (300g),
chopped finely

150g lean minced lamb

150g white long-grain rice

2 tablespoons pine nuts

6 tablespoons finely chopped
fresh flat-leaf parsley

2 tablespoons finely chopped
fresh dill

2 tablespoons finely chopped
fresh mint

2 tablespoons lemon juice

250ml water

500g preserved vine leaves

250ml water, extra

1 tablespoon lemon juice, extra

200g natural yogurt

1 Heat oil in large saucepan, add onion; cook, stirring, until softened. Add mince; cook, stirring, until mince is browned. Stir in rice and pine nuts. Add herbs, juice and the water. Bring to the boil; reduce heat, simmer, covered, about 10 minutes or until water is absorbed and rice is partially cooked. Cool.

2 Rinse vine leaves in cold water. Drop leaves into a large saucepan of boiling water, in batches, for a few seconds, transfer to colander; rinse under cold water, drain well.

3 Place a vine leaf, smooth side down on work surface, trim large stem. Place a heaped teaspoon of rice mixture in centre. Fold stem end and sides over filling; roll up firmly. Line medium heavy-based saucepan with a few vine leaves, place rolls, close together, seam side down on leaves.

4 Pour the extra water over top of rolls; cover rolls with any remaining vine leaves. Place a plate on top of the leaves to keep rolls under the water during cooking.

Cover pan tightly, bring to the boil; reduce heat, simmer, over very low heat, 1½ hours. Remove from heat; stand, covered about 2 hours or until all the liquid has been absorbed.

5 Serve cold with combined extra juice and yogurt.

prep + cook time 3 hours
+ standing time
serves 10
nutritional count per serving
7.6g fat; 690kJ (165 cal)

tips Use any torn or damaged leaves to line the base of the pan and to cover the rolls. If you don't have enough vine leaves to cover the rolls in the pan, use a circle of baking parchment, then top with the plate. Dolmades are best made a day ahead; store, covered, in the refrigerator.

MINI ROASTED PEPPER & GOAT'S CHEESE TERRINES

3 large red peppers (1kg)
360g ricotta cheese, chopped coarsely
250g firm goat's cheese, chopped coarsely
3 tablespoons finely chopped fresh chives
2 tablespoons lemon juice
1 clove garlic, crushed
chopped fresh chives, extra

spinach & walnut pesto
20g finely grated parmesan cheese
100g baby spinach leaves
25g roasted walnuts
1 clove garlic, quartered
60ml olive oil
2 tablespoons lemon juice
1 tablespoon water

1 Preheat oven to 240°C/220°C fan-assisted. Grease six holes of eight-hole (125ml) mini loaf pan. Line base and two long sides of each hole with a strip of baking parchment, extending 5cm over sides.
2 Halve peppers; discard seeds and membranes. Place on oven tray; roast, skin-side up, about 15 minutes or until skin blisters and blackens. Cover with cling film for 5 minutes then peel away skin. Cut pepper into strips; line base and two long sides of pan holes with pepper strips, extending 2cm over edges.
3 Combine remaining ingredients in medium bowl; spoon cheese mixture into pan holes, pressing down firmly. Fold pepper strips over to enclose filling. Cover; refrigerate 1 hour.
4 Meanwhile, make spinach and walnut pesto.
5 Carefully remove terrines from pan holes; cut into slices and serve with spinach and walnut pesto; sprinkle with chopped fresh chives.

spinach & walnut pesto Process cheese, spinach, nuts and garlic until chopped finely. With motor operating, gradually add combined oil, juice and the water in a thin, steady stream; process until pesto is smooth.

prep + cook time 45 minutes + refrigeration time
makes 6
nutritional count per terrine 26.8g fat; 1417kJ (339 cal)

TINY SWEET TREATS

ROSÉ WINE JELLIES

75g caster sugar
42g powdered gelatine
750ml rosé wine
2 tablespoons double cream
100g white eating chocolate,
    chopped coarsely
36 rose petals

1 Sprinkle sugar and gelatine over 250ml of the wine in large heatproof jug; stand jug in medium saucepan of simmering water. Stir until gelatine dissolves.
2 Stir remaining wine into gelatine mixture. Pour mixture into two 18-hole (20ml) flexible jelly moulds. Refrigerate 3 hours or until firm.
3 Stir cream and chocolate in small heatproof bowl over small saucepan of simmering water until smooth. Refrigerate about 30 minutes, stirring occasionally, until spreadable.
4 Half-fill shallow baking dish with boiling water; stand jelly moulds in dish about 2 seconds or until jelly begins to come away from side of moulds. Carefully unmould jellies onto tray. Pipe or spoon chocolate mixture onto jellies; top with rose petals.

prep + cook time 20 minutes + refrigeration time
makes 36
nutritional count per jelly 1.3g fat; 186kJ (45 cal)
tip Rose, violet, nasturtium and pansy petals are all edible and make beautiful additions to recipes.

PISTACHIO & ORANGE BLOSSOM MACAROONS

45g unsalted roasted pistachios
3 egg whites
55g caster sugar
green food colouring
200g icing sugar
90g ground almonds
1 tablespoon icing sugar, extra
60ml double cream
150g white eating chocolate,
   chopped coarsely
4 teaspoons orange blossom
   water

1 Grease oven trays; line with baking parchment.
2 Process pistachios until ground finely.
3 Beat egg whites in small bowl with electric mixer until soft peaks form. Add caster sugar and a few drops of colouring, beat until sugar dissolves; transfer mixture to large bowl. Fold in 35g of the ground pistachios, sifted icing sugar and ground almonds, in two batches.
4 Spoon mixture into piping bag fitted with 2cm plain tube. Pipe 4cm rounds about 2cm apart onto trays. Tap trays on work surface so macaroons spread slightly. Dust with extra sifted icing sugar; sprinkle with remaining ground pistachios. Stand 30 minutes.
5 Meanwhile, preheat oven to 150°C/130°C fan-assisted.
6 Bake macaroons for about 20 minutes. Cool on trays.
7 Bring cream to the boil in small saucepan, remove from heat; add chocolate, stir until smooth. Stir in orange blossom water. Refrigerate until spreadable.

8 Sandwich macaroons with chocolate filling.

prep + cook time 40 minutes + standing and refrigeration time
makes 16
nutritional count per macaroon 9g fat; 752kJ (180 cal)
tip Unfilled macaroons will keep in an airtight container for about a week. Fill just before serving.

CARAMEL CASHEW TARTS

150g roasted unsalted cashews
1 tablespoon cornflour
165g brown sugar
2 tablespoons golden syrup
50g butter, melted
2 eggs
2 tablespoons double cream
1 teaspoon vanilla extract

pastry
185g plain flour
55g caster sugar
125g chilled butter, chopped
　　coarsely
1 egg yolk
2 teaspoons water

cinnamon cream
300ml whipping cream
1 tablespoon icing sugar
1 teaspoon ground cinnamon

1 Make pastry.
2 Grease two 12-hole (80ml) muffin pans. Roll pastry between sheets of baking parchment to 3mm thickness; cut out 24 x 8cm rounds. Press rounds into pan holes; prick bases all over with fork. Refrigerate 20 minutes.
3 Preheat oven to 200°C/180°C fan-assisted.
4 Bake pastry cases 10 minutes. Cool. Reduce temperature to 160°C/140°C fan-assisted.
5 Combine nuts and cornflour in medium bowl; stir in sugar, syrup, butter, egg, cream and vanilla extract. Divide filling among pastry cases. Bake about 15 minutes; cool. Refrigerate 30 minutes.
6 Meanwhile, beat ingredients for cinnamon cream in small bowl with electric mixer until soft peaks are formed.
7 Serve tarts with cinnamon cream.

pastry Process flour, sugar and butter until coarse. Add egg yolk and the water; process until combined. Knead on floured surface until smooth. Cover; refrigerate 30 minutes.

prep + cook time 45 minutes + refrigeration and cooling time
makes 24
nutritional count per tart
15.2g fat; 932kJ (223 cal)
tip If pastry is too dry, add 2 teaspoons of water with the egg yolk.

LIME MERINGUE TARTLETS

2 eggs, separated
2 tablespoons caster sugar
1 teaspoon finely grated lime rind
1½ tablespoons lime juice
20g butter
20 x 4cm ready-made pastry
  cases
110g caster sugar, extra
50g shredded coconut

1 Combine egg yolks, sugar, rind, juice and butter in small heatproof bowl. Stir over small saucepan of simmering water until mixture thickens slightly and coats the back of a spoon; remove from heat. Cover; refrigerate curd until cold.
2 Preheat oven to 220°C/200°C fan-assisted.
3 Divide curd among pastry cases; place on oven tray.
4 Beat egg whites in small bowl with electric mixer until soft peaks form; gradually beat in extra sugar until dissolved. Fold in 35g of the coconut. Spoon meringue evenly over curd to enclose filling; sprinkle with remaining coconut.
5 Bake tarts about 3 minutes or until meringue is browned lightly.

prep + cook time 40 minutes + refrigeration time
serves 20
nutritional count per tartlet 6g fat 46 kJ (110 cal)
tips Make sure you spread the meringue right out to the pastry – where the curd meets the side of the cases. The meringue should be barely browned, just kissed by the heat.

CHOC-TOFFEE NUTS

110g slivered almonds
110g coarsely chopped roasted
    hazelnuts
55g caster sugar
1 tablespoon orange juice
2 teaspoons finely grated
    orange rind
250g dark eating chocolate,
    melted

1 Preheat oven to 180°C/160°C fan-assisted. Line two 12-hole (20ml) mini muffin pans with paper cases.

2 Combine nuts, sugar and juice in small bowl. Spread mixture onto greased oven tray. Bake, stirring occasionally, about 15 minutes or until browned lightly.

3 Remove nut mixture from oven; add rind. Stir to combine rind and break up nut mixture. Cool.

4 Combine nut mixture with chocolate in medium bowl. Divide mixture among paper cases. Stand at room temperature until set.

prep + cook time 35 minutes + cooling and standing time
makes 24
nutritional count per piece
8.4g fat; 514kJ (123 cal)

tip We used freeform paper cases made by pushing an 8cm square of baking parchment into greased pan holes.

MINI TOFFEE APPLES

2 medium red apples (300g)
1 tablespoon lemon juice
660g caster sugar
250ml water

1 Preheat oven to 100°C/80°C fan-assisted. Grease two 12-hole (20ml) mini muffin pans.
2 Cut unpeeled apples into 0.5cm cubes; combine in small bowl with juice. Spread apple onto baking-parchment-lined oven tray. Bake, uncovered, about 40 minutes or until dried.
3 Meanwhile, stir sugar and the water in medium heavy-based saucepan over heat until sugar dissolves. Bring to the boil; boil about 10 minutes, without stirring, or until toffee turns golden brown. Remove pan from heat; allow bubbles to subside.
4 Divide apple among pan holes. Pour toffee slowly over apple; cool toffees about 10 minutes.
5 Cut each lolly stick in half. Position half a stick, cut-side down, in centre of each toffee; cool. Using sharp, pointed knife, carefully insert down one side of each pan hole to loosen toffee from edge of pan.

prep + cook time 40 minutes + cooling time
makes 24
nutritional count per toffee apple 0g fat; 489kJ (117 cal)
tips You need 12 lolly sticks for this recipe. Gently twist the sticks then pull to remove toffees from pan. Using a saucepan with a pouring lip makes it easy to pour the hot toffee into the pans.

GLOSSARY

arborio rice small, round-grain rice well suited to absorb large amount of liquid; especially suitable for risottos.

bicarbonate of soda also called baking soda.

black onion seeds also called nigella or kalonji seeds; are angular seeds, black on the outside and creamy within, having a sharp nutty flavour.

buttermilk fresh low-fat milk cultured to give a slightly sour, tangy taste; low-fat yogurt or milk can be substituted.

caperberries the fruit formed after caper buds have flowered, caperberries are milder in taste than capers. They marry well with seafood dishes and look great on an antipasto platter. Sold pickled with stalks intact, they are available from most delicatessens.

cheese

brie soft-ripened cow's-milk cheese with a delicate, creamy texture and a rich, sweet taste. Best served at room temperature, brie should have a bloomy white rind and creamy, voluptuous centre which becomes runny with ripening.

cheddar the most common cow's milk cheese; should be aged and hard.

feta a crumbly textured goat's- or sheep's-milk cheese with a sharp, salty taste.

goat's made from goat's milk, goat's cheese has an earthy, strong taste. Can be purchased in both soft and firm textures, in various shapes and sizes, sometimes rolled in ash or herbs.

mozzarella a semi-soft cheese with a delicate, fresh taste; has a low melting point and stringy texture when hot.

parmesan a sharp-tasting, dry, hard cheese, made from skimmed or semi-skimmed milk and aged for at least a year.

ricotta a soft, sweet, moist, white, cow's-milk cheese with a low fat content and a slightly grainy texture. The name roughly translates as 'cooked again' and refers to ricotta's manufacture from whey that is itself a by-product of other cheese making.

stilton an English blue veined cheese, known for its characteristic strong smell and taste. Also available in a white variety.

cornflour also known as cornstarch; used as a thickening agent in cooking.

crème fraîche a mature fermented cream having a slightly tangy flavour and velvety rich texture; similar in thickness to soured cream.

fish sauce also called nam pla or nuoc nam; made from pulverised salted fermented fish, mostly anchovies. Has a pungent smell and strong taste; use sparingly.

flour

buckwheat a herb in the same plant family as rhubarb; not a cereal so it is gluten-free. Available as flour, granules or groats (whole roasted kernels).

plain an all-purpose flour made from wheat.

self-raising plain flour sifted with baking powder (a raising agent consisting mainly of 2 parts cream of tartar to 1 part bicarbonate of soda) in the proportion of 150g flour to 2 level teaspoons baking powder.

ghee clarified butter; with the milk solids removed, this fat can be heated to a very high temperature without burning.

golden syrup a by-product of refined sugarcane; pure maple syrup or honey can be substituted.

Japanese soy sauce an all-purpose low-sodium sauce made from fermented soy beans but with more wheat content than its Chinese counterparts. Possibly the best table soy and the one to choose if you only want one variety.

mustard

black mustard seeds also known as brown mustard seeds.

hot English among the strongest, hottest mustards, made from ground yellow mustard seeds and water but no vinegar.

wholegrain also known as seeded. A French-style coarse-grain mustard made from crushed mustard seeds and Dijon-style French mustard.

orange blossom water also known as orange flower water, concentrated flavouring made from orange blossoms.

paprika ground dried red pepper; available sweet, smoked or hot.

pastry

filo chilled or frozen tissue-thin pastry sheets that are very versatile, lending themselves to both sweet and savoury dishes. Filo pastry tends to dry out quickly – it's best to cover it with a damp cloth while you're working with it.

puff a crisp, light pastry; layers of dough and fat are folded and rolled many times making many layers. When baked, it becomes a high, crisp, flaky pastry. Butter puff pastry uses butter for the shortening, whereas puff pastry uses a commercially made blend of vegetable and animal fats.

shortcrust a tender, crunchy, melt in the mouth buttery pastry. Once baked it is a light, crumbly and easily broken.

pine nuts also known as pignoli; small, cream-coloured kernels obtained from the cones of different varieties of pine trees.

prosciutto a salted-cured, air-dried (unsmoked), pressed ham; usually sold in paper-thin slices, ready to eat.

rye bread made with flour ground from rye grain, it can be light or dark in colour and is denser than bread made from wheat flour. It is higher in fibre than white bread and stronger in flavour.

sesame seeds black and white are the most common of these tiny oval seeds; a good source of calcium.

tabasco sauce brand name of an extremely fiery sauce made from vinegar, hot red peppers and salt.

vinegar

rice wine a colourless vinegar made from fermented rice and flavoured with sugar and salt. Also called seasoned rice vinegar; sherry can be substituted.

sherry mellow wine vinegar named for its colour.

wine based on fermented red or white wine.

wasabi an Asian horseradish used to make the pungent, green-coloured paste traditionally served with Japanese raw fish dishes. Available, in powdered or paste form, from supermarkets and Asian food stores.

yeast a raising agent used in dough making. Dried (7g sachets) and fresh compressed (20g blocks) yeast can almost always be substituted one for the other when yeast is called for; allow 15g compressed yeast to 2 teaspoons (7g) dried yeast if substituting.

INDEX

CONVERSION CHARTS

measures

One metric tablespoon holds 20ml; one metric teaspoon holds 5ml.

All cup and spoon measurements are level. The most accurate way of measuring dry ingredients is to weigh them. When measuring liquids, use a clear glass or plastic jug with metric markings.

We use large eggs with an average weight of 60g.

dry measures

METRIC	IMPERIAL
15g	½oz
30g	1oz
60g	2oz
90g	3oz
125g	4oz (¼lb)
155g	5oz
185g	6oz
220g	7oz
250g	8oz (½lb)
280g	9oz
315g	10oz
345g	11oz
375g	12oz (¾lb)
410g	13oz
440g	14oz
470g	15oz
500g	16oz (1lb)
750g	24oz (1½lb)
1kg	32oz (2lb)

liquid measures

METRIC	IMPERIAL
30ml	1 fluid oz
60ml	2 fluid oz
100ml	3 fluid oz
125ml	4 fluid oz
150ml	5 fluid oz
190ml	6 fluid oz
250ml	8 fluid oz
300ml	10 fluid oz
500ml	16 fluid oz
600ml	20 fluid oz
1000ml (1 litre)	32 fluid oz

length measures

3mm	⅛in
6mm	¼in
1cm	½in
2cm	¾in
2.5cm	1in
5cm	2in
6cm	2½in
8cm	3in
10cm	4in
13cm	5in
15cm	6in
18cm	7in
20cm	8in
23cm	9in
25cm	10in
28cm	11in
30cm	12in (1ft)

oven temperatures

These are fan-assisted temperatures. If you have a conventional oven (ie. not fan-assisted), increase temperatures by 10–20°.

	°C (CELSIUS)	°F (FAHRENHEIT)	GAS MARK
Very low	100	210	½
Low	130	260	1–2
Moderately low	140	280	3
Moderate	160	325	4–5
Moderately hot	180	350	6
Hot	200	400	7–8
Very hot	220	425	9